TRUST
Is a Must

Finding the Quiet Strength of God's Peace!

TRUST
Is a Must

ROY LESSIN

SWEETWATFR STILL PUBLISHING
SALEM, ARKANSAS

Cover design and interior layout by Milk n Honey Design, AR, USA

TRUST IS A MUST

First published as *Fret Busters* in 2015 by Harvest House Publishers. This fully revised edition published in 2025 by Sweetwater Still Publishing, Arkansas USA.

ISBN: 978-1-7356345-9-3
LCCN: 2025941063

25 26 27 28 / 5 4 3 2 1

"And those who know Your name will put their trust in You; For You, LORD, have not forsaken those who seek You."

(Psalm 9:10)

This book is dedicated to every seeking heart who desires to put their trust in the Lord, and to keep it there no matter the circumstances.

Roy Lessin

Come to Me

Separate yourself
unto Me,
Know Me,
Trust Me...

I am your God.
I dwell with you,
Walk with you,
Welcome you.

You are my child.
I am your Father.

(Based upon 2 Cor. 6:16-18)

I Am God!

Lord, You are who You say You are.

You do what You say You do.
There is no other!

You are the highest, the greatest,
the best. You have no weakness,
no lack, and no equal.

You are my God and my
Heavenly Father.

I find comfort in Your nearness,
security in Your voice, courage in
Your strength, and hope in
Your promises.

You are enough. More than enough!
You are with me. You are my refuge.
I am safe in Your care.

All-in-All

All throughout the Scriptures God proclaims and demonstrates who He is and what He can do. God is all-in-all! He has no lack, no faults, no weaknesses, no limitations, and no failures.

The plan of our salvation is His plan; the work of our salvation is His work; the gift of our salvation is His gift.

Every grace comes from Him—all that we have, we have freely received from His generous hand.

How should we respond to His greatness and abounding generosity? Our response is to *be* with Him, *learn* of Him, *love* Him, and to *trust* Him with all our hearts.

If we obey God without fully trusting Him and knowing His heart, we will struggle in our obedience.

It has been said, "Perfect obedience would be perfect happiness, if only we had perfect confidence in the One we were obeying."

We can *fully* put our trust in what God has said and promised, who He is, what He has done, what He is doing, and what He will do.

HE
will NOT FAIL,
for there is
NO FAILURE *in*
HIM.

Even Though

Take His hand, even though it means letting go of what you are holding on to.

Please His heart, even though it may not please others.

Wait for His time, even though your desire is to get it done now.

Obey His Word, even though you hear something different that is popular.

Follow His path, even though you see a valley ahead.

Trust His wisdom, even though you want to do it differently.

Give Him praise, even though you are going through something unpleasant.

Be at rest, even though you have every reason to worry or fear.

"Uphold me according to Your word, that I may live; And do not let me be ashamed of my hope. Hold me up, and I shall be safe, And I shall observe Your statutes continually."
(Psalm 119:116-117)

Why Worry?

"Stop worrying about what you will eat, drink, or wear. Isn't life more than food and the body more than clothes? Look at the birds. They don't plant, harvest, or gather the harvest into barns. Yet, your heavenly Father feeds them. Aren't you worth more than they?

"Can any of you add a single hour to your life by worrying? And why worry about clothes? Notice how the flowers grow in the field. They never work or spin yarn for clothes. But I say that not even Solomon in all his majesty was dressed like one of these flowers...So how much more will He clothe you people who have so little faith?

"Don't ever worry and say, 'What are we going to eat?' or 'What are we going to drink?' or 'What are we going to wear?' Everyone is concerned about these things, and your heavenly Father certainly knows you need all of them. But first, be concerned about His kingdom and what has His approval. Then all these things will be provided for you."
(Matthew 6:25-33 GW)

Open to Peace!

How is it possible to live free from worry? Living free from worry does not mean that our needs will disappear, but that our needs will be met by God who is our provider.

When we stay focused on what our needs are, we open our hearts to worry; when we stay focused on who God is, we open our hearts to peace.

I AM *here.*

ALL that I AM *is here...*

ALL My love *is here,*

ALL My goodness *is here,*

ALL My righteousness *is here,*

ALL My grace *is here,*

ALL My strength *is here,*

ALL My ways, My works,

My wisdom, My wonders

are here!

Is there ANYTHING

too hard FOR ME?

He Gives Rest

Thankfully, we have a Master who not only gives us rest *from* our labor, but He also gives us rest *in* our labor. We have a Master who is our rest.

"Then Jesus said, 'Let's go off by ourselves
to a quiet place and rest awhile.'"
(Mark 6:31 NLT)

"Come to me, all of you who are weary and
carry heavy burdens, and I will give you rest."
(Matthew 11:28 NLT)

"Rest in the Lord."
(Psalm 37:7)

Will Be!

"The night is almost gone; the day of salvation will soon be here." (Romans 13:12 NLT)

"Will be!"
Not, "Might be."
Not, "Could be."

What a blessed reality; what a magnificent truth; what a hope-filled promise from the God of all hope! His "will be" is our hope in dark times, troubled times, uncertain times, and changing times.

What will be?
He will be!
His return will be!
His reign will be!
Righteousness will be!
Your place with Him will be!
Your inheritance will be!

Receive Peace

"We have peace with God through our
Lord Jesus Christ." (Romans 5:1)

Father, I have received peace *from* You
and peace *with* You because of Your
Son's sacrifice for me. It is amazing to
know that all is well with my soul, that all
has been made right in my relationship
with You, and that I have been accepted
in *the beloved* and adopted into Your
family. I know that the enemies of peace
are not the friends of Your will. You are
the God of peace, the provider of peace,
and the One who maintains my peace.

Your peace is my safe place, my
sheltered place, and my abiding place.

Your peace is my pathway—may every
step be guided by Your peace, may every
decision be governed by Your peace, and
may every act of service be guarded by
Your peace.

Let Your peace mark my footsteps, empower my words, and shield my heart.

Peace is in Your voice, peace is in Your heart, peace is in Your kingdom, peace is in Your truth, and peace is in Your purposes. Thank You for keeping me in perfect peace.

I can go
when God sends me.
I can rejoice
when standing still.
I am patient
and contented,
when I'm resting
in His will.

Prayer of Release

"I know the one in whom I trust, and I am sure that he is able to guard what I have entrusted to him until the day of his return."
(2 Timothy 1:12 NLT)

Heavenly Father, I release to You the burdens that I have been carrying, burdens that You never intended for me to carry. I cast all my cares upon You—all my worries and all my fears. You have told me not to be anxious about anything, but rather to bring everything to You in prayer, with thankfulness.

Father, calm my restless spirit, quiet my anxious heart, and still my troubling thoughts with the assurance that You are in control.

I let go of my grip upon the things I have been hanging onto. With opened hands I come to You. I release to Your will all that I am trying to manipulate.

I release to Your authority all that I am trying to control; I release to Your timing all that I have been striving to make happen.

I thank You for Your promise to sustain me, preserve me, and guard all that I have entrusted to Your keeping. Protect my heart and mind with Your peace, the peace that passes all understanding. Father, may Your will be done in my life, in Your time, and in Your way.

(Scriptures: Psalm 55:22, 1 Peter 5:7, Philippians 4:6, Matthew 6, Isaiah 26:3, Luke 11:2)

He Cares

"Casting the whole of your care [all your anxieties, all your worries, all your concerns, once and for all] on Him, for He cares for you affectionately and cares about you watchfully."
(1 Peter 5:7 AMPC)

Once we give our worries to God, He doesn't want us to worry about how He is going to take care of them. He is Almighty, and He knows how to take care of us. We can leave the details to Him.

Keep His
HOPE
in your heart.

Keep His
DAY
OF SALVATION
in your planner.

Keep His
LIGHT
in your eye.

Letting Go

What do we do with the things we can't fix, the decisions we can't control, the events we can't attend, the opportunities we can't respond to, or the circumstances we can't change? Should we get angry, frustrated, anxious, disappointed, *grumbly,* or discouraged?

Thankfully, there is a better response! The response is like a two-sided coin. On one side the coin says "Let Go," and on the other side it says "Let God."

"Letting Go" is when you find release;
> "Letting God" is when your heart finds peace.

"Letting Go" is when you seek His best;
> "Letting God" is when your heart finds rest.

"Letting Go" is when you choose His will;
> "Letting God" is when your heart is still.

"God, I have let go, but I'm falling!" I cried out in fear.

"Do not be troubled," He lovingly replied, *"I am underneath you, and you are falling into My everlasting arms!"*

God is too *powerful* to lead you to a place of defeat;
Too *wise* to bring wrong things into your life;
Too *caring* to leave you without comfort;
Too *observant* to miss a detail;
Too *loving* to withhold anything that is good.

A Quiet Heart

There is something important we can learn from the way of a mother with a young child who is frightened. The response of a young child to fear is not a whimper, but a wail. The mother's response is not casual or indifferent, but one that is instant and intense. Love moves into action, not with explanations or reasoning, but with everything in its power to quiet, to comfort, and to reassure. The arms of the mother's embrace speak louder than any words the child could hear in that moment of fear.

The mother's voice is also soothing and quieting, "Shh, it's okay...mommy's here. It's okay." These words are all the child needs to know. Her gentle words and loving arms bring the assurance that helps the child to become calm.

The words God speaks in Psalm 46:10-11 can be likened to the words of a caring mother to her fearful child. The language is simple, the words are few, the impact is instant, and the result is profound. His words tell us all we need to know to settle us, still our fears, quiet our hearts, and reassure us. Hear His reassuring voice:

"Be still, release all your concerns, and quiet your heart; it's okay, I am here and you are safe in the shelter of My arms."

"Be still, and know that I am God... The LORD of hosts is with us; The God of Jacob is our refuge." (Psalm 46:10-11)

Good Burdens

"An aged, weary woman, carrying a heavy basket, got aboard a train, and when seated she did not let go of her heavy basket. The kind voice of a man sitting next to her spoke these words, 'Lay down your burden, madam; the train will carry both it and you.'"
THE SILVER LINING, J. H. JOWETT

In the illustration above, the aged woman's basket and its contents were not a bad thing. The basket may have contained the food items needed to feed her family that day. It was the weight of the basket that made the woman weary.

Is there something in your life that has become a burden? It may be a good thing, and the right thing for you to do, but there may be a weight associated with it that is making you weary. The Lord may not want you to cast away the good thing, but He does want you to cast the care of it upon Him and let Him carry it.

Perhaps the weight is associated with your job. The Lord may want you to keep the job, but not carry the weight of "striving in your work to get ahead."

Perhaps the weight is associated with a ministry. The Lord may want you to continue in that ministry, but not carry the weight of "trying to please people."

Perhaps the weight is associated with a difficult situation. The Lord may want you to press through the difficulty, but not carry the weight of "doing it in your own strength."

The Lord desires to release you from every burden that would weigh you down, make your heart heavy, or rob you of the strength you need to do His will. He will sustain you. He is able to carry both you and the weight of your burden!

"Cast thy burden upon the LORD, and He shall sustain thee: He shall never suffer the righteous to be moved." (Psalm 55:22 KJV)

He Gives Freely

"The Spirit and the bride say, 'Come!' Let those who hear this say, 'Come!' Let those who are thirsty come! Let those who want the water of life take it as a gift." (Revelation 22:17 GW)

God gives to you freely out of the riches of His grace, the bounty of His goodness, the kindness of His favor, the depths of His love, the tender ministry of His Spirit, and the blessings that abound to you in His Son, Jesus Christ—all of which have no limitations and can never be depleted. By faith, receive from Him today, for He is the endless supply!

Needy? Come and ask.
Seeking? Come and find.
Thirsty? Come and drink.
Hungry? Come and dine.
Hurt? Come and heal.
Weary? Come and rest.

THERE
WILL NEVER
BE A TIME
when you will find
GOD'S POWER
inadequate,
HIS LOVE
indifferent,
HIS GRACE
insufficient.

I Need

Jesus, You spoke the word and the storm became still.

Lord, I need a word like that.
(Mark 4:39)

Jesus, those who touched the hem of Your garment were made whole.

Lord, I need a healing like that.
(Mark 6:56)

Jesus, You gave the spiritually hungry living Bread.

Lord, I need to be fed like that.
(John 6:48-51)

Jesus, You placed Your hands upon the children and blessed them.

Lord, I need a touch like that.
(Mark 10:16)

Jesus, You blessed the bread and the wine as You communed with Your disciples.

Lord, I need fellowship like that.
(Mark 14:22-24)

Jesus, You said You go before Your sheep and they follow You.

Lord, I need guidance like that.
(John 10:1-4)

Jesus, You promised a place in Your Father's house to those with troubled hearts.

Lord, I need assurance like that.
(John 14:27)

Jesus, You lived to please Your Father.

Lord, I need a relationship like that.
(John 8:29)

Precious, Simple Trust

"Behold, God is my salvation; I will trust and
not be afraid." (Isaiah 12:2 KJV)

Believe that you are in His heart and
that your interests are in His hands. Have
faith in His wisdom to guide, in His love
to direct, in His power to sustain, and in
His faithfulness to fulfill every promise
that now relates to your best welfare and
happiness.

"My times are in Your hand." (Psalm 31:15)

"Let this precious truth rid your mind of all needless, anxious care for the present or the future. Exercising simple faith in God, 'Do not be anxious about anything.' Learn to be content with your present lot, with God's dealings with, and His disposal of, you. You are just where His providence has, in its inscrutable but all-wise and righteous decision, placed you.

"It may be a position painful, irksome, trying, but it is right. Oh, yes! It is right. Only aim to glorify Him in it. Wherever you are placed, God has a work for you to do, a purpose through you to be accomplished, in which He blends your happiness with His glory...live a life of daily dependence upon God...it saves from many a desponding feeling, from many a corroding care, from many an anxious thought, from many a sleepless night."

OCTAVIUS WINSLOW

He Did Not Say

The only reason to fear or worry is *if* the Lord had said:

1. Lay up treasures on earth, for there are no treasures in heaven.
2. Be anxious about life, for God doesn't know anything about you.
3. The most important thing in life is what you possess, so get more.
4. Your Father doesn't care for you; you are on your own.
5. Seek what the world seeks; that is where true riches are.
6. Be anxious about tomorrow; it's good to have things pile up.
7. God cannot look after the practical details of life; save yourself.

Since He *hasn't* said these things, continue to walk in peace.

"Let your character or moral disposition be free from love of money [including greed, avarice, lust, and craving for earthly possessions] and be satisfied with your present [circumstances and with what you have]; for He [God] Himself has said, I will not in any way fail you nor give you up nor leave you without support.

"[I will] not, [I will] not, [I will] not in any degree leave you helpless nor forsake nor let [you] down (relax My hold on you)! [Assuredly not!]

"So we take comfort and are encouraged and confidently and boldly say, 'The Lord is my Helper; I will not be seized with alarm [I will not fear or dread or be terrified]. What can man do to me?'" (Hebrews 13:5-6 AMPC)

Count on God

"We have been brought through deep troubles, yet the Lord has not forsaken us. Anything human—plans, devices, fears—man naturally indulges in; but to trust in God implicitly is, foolishly enough, only a kind of last resource. But it is when we come to that, that we see the folly of anything else." MACKAY

You can count on God.

His words are truth; He cannot lie.

His character is flawless; He does what He says He will do.

He never fails. He never errs.

"Uphold me according to Your word, that I may live; And do not let me be ashamed of my hope. Hold me up, and I shall be safe, And I shall observe Your statutes continually."
(Psalm 119:116-117)

THE
LORD
Himself
*will fight
for you.*

Just stay calm.

(Exodus 14:14 NLT)

Grace We Need

There is a grace God gives you when it is His time for you to do His will, and there is a grace that He gives you when you are waiting on His will to be done. His grace includes the fruit of patience and the peace of contentment.

Patience says, "I can wait for His time."

Contentment says, "I am at peace with the way things are at the moment."

Patience allows you to wait without striving; contentment allows you to wait without complaint.

"Ask, and you will receive. Search and you will find. Knock and the door will be opened for you. Everyone who asks will receive. The one who searches will find, and for the one who knocks, the door will be opened. If your child asks you for bread, would any of you give him a stone? Or if your child asks for a fish, would you give him a snake? Even though you're evil, you know how to give good gifts to your children.

So how much more will your Father in heaven give good things to those who ask Him?" (Matthew 7:7-11 GW)

Though everyone fails you, God remains faithful. (2 Timothy 2:13)

Though everyone speaks lies, God remains true. (Hebrews 4:1)

Though all things lose their luster, God remains glorious. (2 Corinthians 3:11)

Though all would forsake you, God remains with you. (Haggai 2:5)

Though the world grows exceedingly troubled, God remains in control. (Hebrews 4:9)

Let His Peace Rule

God wants you to move through this day with a *quiet heart,*

An inward assurance that He is in control,

A peaceful certainty that your life is in His hands,

A deep trust in His plan and purposes,

An abiding hope in His promises,

And a thankful disposition toward all that He allows.

"Let the peace of God rule in your hearts."
(Colossians 3:15)

He Goes Before

"For you shall not go out with haste, Nor go by flight; For the Lord will go before you, And the God of Israel will be your rear guard."
(Isaiah 52:12)

God's peace and calmness is a mark of our walk when the Holy Spirit is in control of us—sanctifying our thoughts, guiding our steps, directing our decisions, prompting us to move at the right time, and assuring us that He goes before us and takes care of all that is behind.

No Need

There's no need to try and figure everything out; *God is omniscient.*

There's no need to worry about where you are or where you are going; *God is omnipresent.*

There is no need to do things in your own strength; *God is omnipotent.*

"He who did not spare His own Son, but delivered Him up for us all, how shall He not with Him also freely give us all things?" (Romans 8:32)

God did not give up on you when you didn't know Him, and He will certainly not give up on you now that you are His.

"Listen to Me [says the Lord], O house of Jacob, and all the remnant of the house of Israel, you who have been borne by Me from your birth, carried from the womb: Even to your old age I am He, and even to hair white with age will I carry you. I have made, and I will bear; yes, I will carry and will save you." (Isaiah 46:3-4 AMPC)

Let Down Your Wings

"The likeness of the firmament above the heads of the living creatures was like the color of an awesome crystal, stretched out over their heads...and when they stood still, they let down their wings. A voice came from above the firmament that was over their heads; whenever they stood, they let down their wings." (Ezekiel 1:22-25)

"Flapping wings" is a picture of activity. It can be good activity; it can even be activity in the Lord's work. However, we all need those times when we quiet ourselves before the Lord.

"Letting down our wings" means quieting ourselves and being still before the Lord to hear His voice. It is a good thing to be still and know that He is God and to become a good listener.

Benediction

"I pray that you may prosper in every way and [that your body] may keep well, even as [I know] your soul keeps well and prospers."
(3 John 1:2 AMPC)

May all things be well with you—may you do well, choose well, think well, love well, serve well, feel well, and stay well—as you continue to trust in the only One who does all things well.

Confidence
IS NOT BASED
UPON YOU
*having all the resources
needed to take care of*
yourself.

Confidence
IS BASED UPON
the TRUTH that
GOD IS
faithful.

100% Peace!

"Be anxious for nothing, but in everything by prayer and supplication, with thanksgiving, let your requests be made known to God..."
(Philippians 4:6)

How much peace does it take to balance anxiety in our lives? No amount of peace can balance anxiety because there is no balancing point. God wants the peace/anxiety ratio in our lives to be: peace 100% and anxiety 0%.

Be at peace.

GOD

HAS NOT

forgotten you!

How Much? 100%

"His name shall be called...Prince of Peace."
(Isaiah 9:6)

How much of your care can you cast upon the Lord? All care, all worry, all anxiety, all concerns, and all burdens!

Do it once and for all, and get out of the worrying business. You can hang a banner over your heart that reads: "Under the Management of the Prince of Peace."

"Sing, O heavens! Be joyful, O earth! And break out in singing, O mountains! For the Lord has comforted His people, And will have mercy on His afflicted. But Zion said, 'The Lord has forsaken me, And my Lord has forgotten me.' 'Can a woman forget her nursing child, And not have compassion on the son of her womb? Surely they may forget, Yet I will not forget you. See, I have inscribed you on the palms of My hands; Your walls are continually before Me.'" (Isaiah 49:13-16)

Prayer of Trust

Lord, I trust in You. I believe in You. I hope in You. You are my confidence and my assurance.

I lean upon You, for You are my Rock; I depend upon You, for You are my Provider; I delight in You, for You are the joy of my life.

My heart rests in You; my faith responds to You, and my soul rejoices in You. You are the true God who cannot lie and will not fail. You are the Lord, the Almighty God, and the Creator of all things. You are my Lord, My God, and my Maker.

You are my Keeper, and I am secure; You are my Father, and I am cared for; You are my Counselor and I am guided; You are my shelter and I am safe.

I trust You in life—for the wisdom of Your ways, for the blessings of Your favor, for the sufficiency of Your grace, for the power of Your Spirit, and for the endurance that comes from Your strength.

Lord, I trust in You; my mind trusts in You, my will trusts in You, my soul trusts in You, and from the depths of my being, I trust in You.

Prayer of Peace

Lord Jesus, I thank You that You are the Prince of Peace and that You have promised to give me Your peace.

I receive Your peace, the peace that passes all understanding, the peace that assures me of Your presence, the peace that confirms Your love, and the peace that guards my every thought and each emotion.

Thank You that You have come, not to trouble me, but to give me Your rest; not to confuse me, but to give me clarity; not to bind me, but to free me; not to stress me, but to quiet me.

Thank You for a peace that endures the trial, overcomes the battle, conquers the foe, and keeps me steady through the storm.

Thank You, Lord, for complete peace, for perfect peace, for a peace that keeps my heart from being troubled. Come now and fill me with Your peace.

Thank You for the perfect peace that comes when I put my trust in You. Let it wash over me and flood my innermost being. Show me the ways of peace, keep me in the paths of peace, and guide me in the decisions that lead to peace. Jesus, be my peace today.

(Scriptures: Isaiah 9:6, John 14:27, Luke 1:79, Philippians 4:6-7, Psalm 29:11, Psalm 55:18, Psalm 85:8, Isaiah 26:3, 32:17, 54:10, 57:19, Romans 14:17, 15:33, Colossians 3:15)

He's the One

"It is the Lord Who goes before you; He will [march] with you; He will not fail you or let you go or forsake you; [let there be no cowardice or flinching, but] fear not, neither become broken [in spirit-depressed, dismayed, and unnerved with alarm]." (Deuteronomy 31:8 AMPC)

It is TRUE!

The One who is BEFORE you and with you will not fail you.

The One who is before you and WITH you will not fail you.

The One who is before you and with you WILL NOT FAIL you.

The One who is before you and with you will not fail YOU.

PEACE IS
not the absence of conflict, but
the **PRESENCE** of
Jesus.

Yoked to Rest

"Take my yoke upon you. Let me teach you, because I am humble and gentle at heart, and you will find rest for your souls. For my yoke is easy to bear, and the burden I give you is light." (Matthew 28:29-30)

When you are yoked to Jesus you are not yoked to restlessness, strife, or worry.

"Anxiety in the heart of man causes depression." (Proverbs 12:25)

God is our Father. There is nothing about His character that would create anxiety in the hearts of His children.

If you are anxious about something, ask yourself if you have prayed about it and fully committed it to the Lord.

If you have prayed about it, committed it to the Lord, and are still anxious, begin to thank God in your heart and in your prayers for being in control of the situation.

Prayer, commitment, and thanksgiving open the door to peace. His peace can be there before the answer comes.

"I am the Lord, the God of all flesh; is there anything too hard for Me?" (Jeremiah 32:27 AMPC)

Surrender to His will today and take the dread out of tomorrow. The Psalmist said, "I have not seen the righteous forsaken." Find your rest in Him today, and let God assume the responsibility for all your tomorrows.

Serene Inside

"For I consider that the sufferings of this present time are not worthy to be compared with the glory which shall be revealed in us."
(Romans 8:18)

The peace that God gives you is not circumstantial peace. Being in a hammock at the beach on a warm sunny day is not a picture of God's peace. Remember, the peace in your heart is God's peace; it's there because He's there, not because everything around you is calm and serene.

Even when you are too weary to stand, His arm will always be there to lean upon!

God Can!

"Therefore do not cast away your confidence, which has great reward." (Hebrews 10:35)

Take "I can't" out of your vocabulary and replace it with "God can!" Be full of confidence, not in yourself or what you can do, but in the Lord and what He can do. Your life, once given to God, is in His hands, not yours; you live in His strength, not yours; you depend upon His resources, not your own.

Shalom Blessing

"Then Gideon built an altar there unto the Lord, and called it *Jehovah-Shalom*." (Judges 6:24)

"Shalom" is much more than a casual social greeting—it is a prayer, a blessing, a deep desire, and a benediction packed with the full blessing of God. In Hebrew the word has many significant meanings throughout the Scriptures. The following is a compilation of those meanings:

> May you be whole in body, soul, and spirit as a result of being in harmony with God's will and purpose for your life.
>
> May His peace be your covering, your heart know His fullness, and by His mighty power may you know victory over every enemy.

May He bring to pass the deepest desires of your heart.

May you know the healing power of His presence and the restoration of every broken relationship.

May every need that you face be met by His limitless resources and sufficiency.

May His covenant promises be fulfilled in your life and in your family.

May He bring you the greatest measure of contentment and the deepest satisfaction that your heart can possibly know.

Lasting Peace

"My peace I give unto you; not as the world giveth, give I unto you." (John 14:27)

The peace the world gives comes from the things the world has to offer. Since everything the world has to offer is temporary, the peace the world gives quickly passes away. The peace that Jesus gives comes from who Jesus is, and *everything Jesus is* lasts forever.

Father,
you are the
GOD *of* PEACE–

PEACE *transcending,*
PEACE *defending,*
PEACE *befriending,*
PEACE *descending,*
PEACE *unending.*

Perfectly Peaceful

"The peace of God, which surpasses all under-standing, will guard your hearts and minds through Christ Jesus." (Philippians 4:7)

Perfect peace is not partial peace, but a peace that is complete, full, and unmixed. It is "Shalom" peace—rich in blessings, well-being, and God's favor. It is a peace of "good health" for the mind, the spirit, and the body. Perfect peace will keep you perfectly peaceful.

I Entrust

I trust You *for* all things.
I trust You *with* all things.
I trust You *in* all things.
I trust You *through* all things.
I trust You *above* all things.

Father, I entrust my future into Your hands, for You who are the Beginning and the End, know the end from the beginning; I entrust my hopes into Your hands, for You never lie; I entrust my labors into Your hands, for you are my exceeding great reward; I entrust my life into Your hands, for You are the one who does all things well.

(Scriptures: Psalm 5:11, 7:1, 9:10, 18:2, 20:7, 25:20, 34:22, 36:7, 37:40, 62:8, 91:2, 118:8, Proverbs 3:5-6, Isaiah 46:10, Revelation 1:8)

The Voice

God's voice is the best voice to hear, the most assuring voice to trust, the clearest voice to follow, the wisest voice to obey, and the most recognizable voice to run to—let the voice of God quiet your heart.

"I will hear what God the LORD will speak: for He will speak peace unto His people..."
(Psalm 85:8 KJV)

❦

"You had faith in the creature, and it disappointed you; in earthly good, and it faded away; in your own heart, and it deceived you. Now, have faith in God! Call upon him in your trouble, try Him in your trial, trust Him in your need, and see if He will not honor the faith that honors Him. 'Have faith in God' -oh, what sweet words of Jesus, spoken to allure your weary spirit to its divine and blessed rest."

OCTAVIUS WINSLOW

"The praying spirit breathe,
The watching power impart,
From all entanglements beneath
Call off my anxious heart.
My feeble mind sustain,
By worldly thoughts oppressed;
Appear, and bid me turn again
To my eternal rest."

CHARLES WESLEY

Do NOT worry
means...
do not worry.

"Therefore do not worry..."
(Matthew 6:31)

Who, What, Where?

Who am I? I am God's child! I am a child of grace and mercy. Jesus looked upon me and came to me with healing in His wings—He saw an empty cup and filled it; He saw an unclean vessel and cleansed it; He saw a restless soul and brought it peace; He saw a lost sheep and brought it home; He saw a vain life and gave it meaning; He saw a selfish heart and baptized it in a river of Holy Love.

"My Father, who has given them to Me, is greater than all; and no one is able to snatch them out of My Father's hand." (John 10:29)

In the center of His hand you find the center of His will; in the center of His will you find the center of His peace; in the center of His peace you find the center of His love; in the center of His love you find the center of His heart.

Two Things

"Your own ears will hear him. Right behind you
a voice will say, 'This is the way you should go,'
whether to the right or to the left."
(Isaiah 30:21 NLT)

There are two things that often rob us
of peace: One is incomplete obedience to
the will of God, and the second is going
beyond the will of God. It's important
to go when He says, "Go." It's equally
important to stop when He says, "Stop."

Daily Portion

"And as for his provisions, there was a regular ration given him by the king, a portion for each day, all the days of his life." (2 Kings 25:30)

Trust the Lord for today's portion of:
Daily bread.
Daily grace.
Daily strength.
Daily hope.
Daily joy.
Daily peace.

"Cast all your care upon Him..." (1 Peter 5:7)

How do you cast your care on Him? Get out your "fishing pole of faith." Take all your cares and put them on a hook. Tie the hook to the line on your fishing pole.

Cast the line as far as you can into the sea of God's faithfulness. Cut the line and leave them there.

On

MY ARM

they will

trust.

(Isaiah 51:5)

Faithful Mind

We all need sanctified imaginations. It is easy for us to fret and have our imaginations run wild. In reality, most things don't happen the way we imagined them.

The Bible does not tell us to live by our imaginations. Our imaginations can be a fast track to worry.

Worry says, "What will happen to me? Things seem out of control!"

Faith says, "My life is in God's hands and He is in control."

Perfect Timing

"For we know in part and we prophesy in part. For now we see in a mirror, dimly, but then face to face. Now I know in part, but then I shall know just as I also am known."
(1 Corinthians 13:9,12)

Be patient; we don't need to know everything right now. In this life we won't be able to resolve every question, solve every problem, or understand every situation. In time, everything will be made clear.

Things won't always be the way they are right now. We don't need to fret over God's timetable. We will inherit all the promises of God through faith and patience. God knows how and when to bring about change. Trust His timing.

What is It?

"Trust in the Lord, and do good; Dwell in the land, and feed on His faithfulness." (Psalm 37:3)

What is it that the Lord has asked of you? Is it time for you to step out? To be still? To let go? To take up? When you know the next step God wants you to take, you must take it in the full confidence of faith. Never put limits upon yourself as to how much you will obey, and never put limits upon God as to how much He can do.

> Anna J. Lindgren said:
> *"He who depends wholly and unconditionally on God becomes an agent for unlimited possibilities."*

What is possible for you today as one who believes in the Lord?

Jesus said in Mark 9:33:
"All things are possible to the one who believes."

Let us place and keep our complete and unconditional trust in the Lord and joyfully walk with Him along the path of unlimited possibilities.

All Grace

"God is able to make all grace abound toward you." (2 Corinthians 9:8)

Don't let your thoughts take you beyond the place of grace. The thought, "What will happen to me?" can take you outside of grace and open the door for your imagination to fill in the blanks with fear and worry.

You need grace for each thing you face. God is the source of the grace you need, and He will not skimp or hold back the portion you need for today's journey. Tomorrow's grace will be yours tomorrow, and tomorrow's grace will also be more than sufficient.

Proclamation of Hope

"[We] rejoice in hope of the glory of God."
(Romans 5:2)

God, You are glorious! Because of who You are, I have hope in what You have promised to do—my future truly is as bright as the words upon Your lips that proclaim it, as powerful as the strength of Your right hand that performs it.

I am confident there are desirable things ahead because You are good; there are perfect things ahead because You are without fault; there are abundant things ahead because You are generous; there are undefiled things ahead because You are holy; there are amazing things ahead because You are wondrous; there are huge things ahead because Your heart is so big!

Wait and Pray

"You will keep him in perfect peace, Whose mind is stayed on You, Because he trusts in You. Trust in the Lord forever, For in Yah, the Lord, is everlasting strength." (Isaiah 26:3-4)

God won't say or do anything for the purpose of frustrating you, making you anxious, causing you to panic, or filling you with fear.

"Do not fret... it only causes harm."
(Psalm 37:8)

If you don't have peace about what you are doing, stop doing it. Most likely, it is not the right thing to do, or it is not the right time.

Count on God
in everything you do,
every circumstance you're in,
in every need you face,
every decision you make.

NEVER think about
anything APART from
Him.

Has He? Will He?

Has He ever left you?
Will He leave you now?
Has He ever forsaken you?
Will He forsake you now?

"For He Himself has said, "I will never
forsake you." (Hebrews 13:5)

Has He ever failed you?
Will He fail you now?

"Be strong, courageous, and firm; fear not nor
be in terror before them, for it is the Lord your
God Who goes with you; He will not fail you."
(Deuteronomy 31:6 AMPC)

Has He ever stopped watching over you?
Will He watch over you now?

"The Lord keeps watch over you as you come
and go, both now and forever."
(Psalm 121:8 NLT)

Has He ever turned His love away?
Will He turn away from you now?

"The Lord appeared from of old to me [Israel],
saying, 'Yes, I have loved you with an
everlasting love; therefore with loving-kindness have I drawn you and continued My faithfulness to you.'" (Jeremiah 31:3 AMPC)

Has He ever ceased to be faithful?
Will He be faithful now?

"The Lord is faithful; He will strengthen you
and guard you from the evil one."
(2 Thessalonians 3:3)

A Basket of Belief

"But without faith it is impossible to please Him, for he who comes to God must believe that He is, and that He is a rewarder of those who diligently seek Him." (Hebrews 11:6)

The thing that believers do best is *believe*. It is the believer who has much to gather along the way, while the doubter travels with an empty basket.

"Keep and guard your heart with all vigilance and above all that you guard, for out of it flow the springs of life." (Proverbs 4:23 AMPC)

When a thought of anxiety comes knocking on the door of your mind, you can refuse it entrance. If you invite it in, it will have dinner with you, and if it has dinner with you, it will quickly move in and want to spend the night.

Should I?

Should I be anxious, if He has all power?

Should I worry, if He knows all things?

Should I be afraid, if He is always present?

Should I doubt, if His promises are true?

Should I disobey, if His ways are best?

Should I strive, if He gives more grace?

"If God cares so wonderfully for flowers that are here today and thrown into the fire tomorrow, He will certainly care for you."
(Luke 12:28 NLT)

It's His Worry!

There once was a man who worried all the time.

But one day a friend noticed that he had stopped worrying.

"How did you do it?" the friend asked.

"It's simple; I hired a man to do all my worrying for me."

"How much did that cost you?"

"I agreed to pay him a thousand dollars a week."

"How can you pay him? You only make five hundred dollars a week."

"Well," said the man, in a calm voice, "I guess that's his worry!"

To Be Still:

Trust is a must.

"You will keep him in perfect peace, Whose mind is stayed on You, Because he trusts in You. Trust in the Lord forever, For in God the Lord, is everlasting strength." (Isaiah 26:3-4)

Rest works best.

"One hand full of rest is better than two fists full of labor and striving after wind." (Ecclesiastics 4:6 NASB)

Peace brings release.

"He has redeemed my soul in peace from the battle that was against me." (Psalm 55:18)

Never!

He will never forget a promise He has made. (God knows all things.)

He will never promise more than He is able to do. (With God, nothing is impossible.)

He will never promise something He has no intention to do. (God cannot lie.)

He will never fail to fulfill a promise because He has been distracted. (With God there is no shadow of turning.)

You
CAN
TRUST
God's promises
ABSOLUTELY!

Lean Hard

"Child of my love, lean hard,
and let Me feel the pressure
of thy care.

I know thy burden, for I
fashioned it—poised it in My
own hand, and made its weight
precisely that which I saw
best for thee. And when I
placed it on thy shrinking
form, I said, 'I shall be near,
and while thou leanest on
Me, this burden shall be
Mine, not thine.'

So shall I keep within My
circling arms the child of my
own love; here lay it down,
nor fear to worry Him who
made, upholds, and guides
the universe.

Yet closer come; thou art not
near enough. Thy care, thyself,
lay both on Me, that I may feel
My child reposing on
My heart.

Thou lovest Me? I doubt it not:
then, loving Me, *lean hard.*"

UNKNOWN

A Defeated Enemy

The enemy of peace has been defeated! Your biggest enemy of peace is not finances, pressures, difficulties, or circumstances of every sort. Your biggest enemy of peace is the devil.

The devil wants you off balance, uncertain, insecure, and troubled about anything and everything happening to you or going on around you.

Before you knew Christ, the devil told you there was no hope for you; when you heard the Gospel, the devil told you that God couldn't be trusted; when you put your trust in the Lord, the devil told you that you didn't trust Him enough.

The devil's plan is simple—he wants to keep you from the truth by tempting you to believe a lie. Lies are thieves that come to steal away the peace of God.

But your enemy has been defeated!

God's will is to keep you in perfect peace. Always stay on God's side and always stay in God's truth. Knowing and believing God's truth will empower you to resist, reject, and refuse to listen to your biggest enemy of peace.

"Keep your mind clear, and be alert. Your opponent the devil is prowling around like a roaring lion as he looks for someone to devour. Be firm in the faith and resist him."
(1 Peter 5:8-9 GW)

Don't Try To:

Figure your way through,
Reason your way through,
Guess your way through,
Feel your way through,
Push your way through,
Manipulate your way through, or
Fake your way through.

Do This Instead:

Trust your way through!

"We do not know what to do, but our eyes are upon You." (2 Chronicles 20:13 AMPC)

Pray your way through!

"Pray at all times (on every occasion, in every season) in the Spirit, with all [manner of] prayer and entreaty. To that end keep alert and watch with strong purpose and perseverance."
(Ephesians 6:18 AMPC)

Believe your way through!

"This is the victory that conquers the world, even our faith." (1 John 5:20 AMPC)

Walk your way through!

"When you walk through the fire of oppression, you will not be burned up; the flames will not consume you. For I am the Lord, your God, the Holy One of Israel, your Savior." (Isaiah 43:2-3 NLT)

Praise your way through!

"So the people shouted when the priests blew the trumpets. And it happened when the people heard the sound of the trumpet, and the people shouted with a great shout, that the wall fell down flat." (Joshua 6:20)

Safe Pastures

Our imaginations are like stallions that need to be broken. If our imaginations are able to run free, they will soon run wild.

Without being under the control of the Holy Spirit, our imaginations can easily mislead us. An unchecked imagination can quickly take us down a road of anxiety and a wide variety of fears.

We need to yield the control our imaginations to the Holy Spirit. He will keep our imaginations feeding in the safe pastures of *Psalm 23*. It is here that Jesus, our Good Shepherd, will lead our imaginations to still waters and quiet resting places.

"The Lord is my Shepherd, I shall not want."
(Psalm 23:1)

HE IS

all that is *good*,
all that is *right*,
all that is *love*.

HE IS

the God *who is
in control* of all
that concerns you!

Hear His Voice

Jesus said that His sheep hear His voice. Here are a few ways to tell His voice from the voice of the enemy:

Jesus doesn't nag, confuse, tease, mock, bully, torment, belittle, degrade, discourage, destroy, harass, or falsify.

Jesus' words free, heal, release, renew, restore, reassure, encourage, comfort, uphold, assure, affirm, edify, and give life.

"The sheep follow him because they recognize his voice. They won't follow a stranger. Instead, they will run away from a stranger because they don't recognize his voice." (John 10:4-5 GW)

Whenever God corrects you, it is always a loving discipline. It is not to drive you away, but to draw you close and bring you back to the place of peace.

God's discipline is always good for us, so that we might share in His holiness.

"No discipline is enjoyable while it is happening—it's painful! But afterward there will be a peaceful harvest of right living for those who are trained in this way."
(Hebrews 12:10-11 NLT)

"The Lord of hosts has sworn, saying, 'Surely, as I have thought and planned, so shall it come to pass, and as I have purposed, so shall it stand— For the Lord of hosts has purposed, and who can annul it? And His hand is stretched out, and who can turn it back?'" (Isaiah 14:24,27 AMPC)

Upon His Shoulders

Jesus, your High Priest, carries you on the strength of His shoulders to bear you up in all your trials; He keeps you close to His heart with the deepest attention and affection; He represents you before the Father with compassionate and sympathetic understanding.

Jesus, your High Priest, strengthens you and helps you; upholds you and undergirds you; carries you and cares for you; represents you and remembers you. He is praying that you will prosper and fully succeed in all the will of God.

You can be assured that Jesus, your faithful High Priest, the One who knows you best and loves you most, holds you close in the depths of His heart, and is carrying you upon the strength of His shoulders.

(Based upon Exodus 28:9-12)

"You prepare a table before me in the presence of my enemies; You anoint my head with oil; My cup runs over." (Psalm 23:5)

"But a certain Samaritan, as he traveled along, came down to where he was; and when he saw him, he was moved with pity and sympathy [for him], And went to him and dressed his wounds, pouring on [them] oil and wine."
(Luke 10:33-34)

His Plan

"I am the Lord, the God of all flesh; is there anything too hard for Me?" (Jer. 32:27 AMPC)

God's plan and care for you have nothing to do with chance, fate, or luck. They're solid, built upon a rock, established upon truth, grounded in love, carried out by omnipotence, secured by providence, watched over by omnipresence, and determined by omniscience.

"We labor to take on ourselves our weary burden, as if He were unable or unwilling to take it for us. He who cannot calmly leave his affairs in God's hand is very likely to be tempted to use wrong means to help himself. Anxiety makes us doubt God's lovingkindness, and our love for Him grows cold. We feel mistrust and grieve the Spirit of God. If we cast each burden as it comes on Him and we are 'careful for nothing' because He undertakes to care for us, it will keep us close to Him."

C.H. SPURGEON

Trustworthy Words

God does not speak lies.

(John 3:33)

God cannot lie because He is holy, and His holiness does not allow Him to lie.

(Psalm 89:35, Titus 1:2)

God's words are wise. He never has to correct Himself or say He misspoke.

(Psalm 19:7)

God's words will not change, because God does not need to correct Himself. He has always had it right from the beginning!

(Psalm 119: 89)

God's words are unshakeable. You can build your life upon them with absolute certainty and confidence.

(Matthew 7:24-25)

He Giveth More

When we have exhausted
Our store of endurance,

When our strength has failed
Ere the day is half done,

When we reach the end
Of our hoarded resources

Our Father's full giving is only begun.

Fear not that thy need shall
exceed His provision.

Our God ever yearns His resources to share;
Lean hard on the arm everlasting, availing;
The Father both thee and thy load will upbear.
His love has no limits,
His grace has no measure,

His power no boundary known unto men;
For out of His infinite riches in Jesus
He giveth, and giveth, and giveth again.

ANNIE JOHNSON FLINT

THE
Healing Oil of Peace,
BEAUTIFUL
in all your *splendor,*
I yield to you
IN FULL SURRENDER.

I take your yoke;
there is no toil.
Lord, pour on me
your healing oil.

He Was, Is, and Will Be

All that He is, He is for You.

Everything that God is today, He has always been, and everything that He has always been, He will always be.

Yesterday, God was with you. Today, God is with you. Tomorrow, God will be with you.

Was He your peace yesterday? He will be your peace today. Is He your peace today? He will be your peace tomorrow. Is He your provider today? He will be your provider tomorrow.

"Care will break the rest of the soul as much as sin does. And there is no hope that we should know the peace that passes all understanding till we have learned the art of shutting the door against the long train of burden—carrying thoughts that are always coming up the hill from the world beneath to fill our spirit with the ring of their feet and the clamor of their cries." F.B. MEYER

Stay Seated!

"God raised us up with Christ and seated us with him in the heavenly realms." (Ephesians 2:6 NIV)

You are seated with Christ. That means you are in a place of rest. To be seated with Him means that you are in the place of His rest and the place of His victory.

His call to you is not *"Work hard to get to where I am"* but rather, *"Live today where I have placed you—with Me at My Father's right hand."*

Are you waiting on God for an answer to something you've prayed about? Stay seated and rest in His answer. Do you have a need you can't meet? Stay seated and rest in His provision. Are you facing a problem you can't solve? Stay seated and rest in His wisdom. Are you wondering how you are going to make it through? Stay seated and rest in His strength.

May You Receive

If you are worried, may you receive the Lord's peace:

"Peace I leave with you; My [own] peace I now give and bequeath to you. Not as the world gives do I give to you.

"Do not let your hearts be troubled, neither let them be afraid. [Stop allowing yourselves to be agitated and disturbed; and do not permit yourselves to be fearful and intimidated and cowardly and unsettled.]"
(John 14:27 AMPC)

If you are wondering, may you receive the Lord's clarity:

"Behold, You desire truth in the inner being; make me therefore to know wisdom in my inmost heart." (Psalm 51:6 AMPC)

If you are wandering, may you receive the Lord's direction:

"And I will bring the blind by a way that they know not; I will lead them in paths that they have not known. I will make darkness into light before them and make uneven places into a plain. These things I have determined to do [for them]; and I will not leave them forsaken."
(Isaiah 42:16 AMPC)

You Can Be Certain:

God created you, shaped you, and brought you into this world:

"But now, thus says the Lord, who created you, O Jacob, And He who formed you, O Israel..."

God wants you to live without fear because the ownership of your life is in His hands, His care, and His keeping. God knows all about you, knows your name, and has set His claim upon you. God is with you and will bring you through every difficult circumstance and trial:

"Fear not, for I have redeemed you... I have called you by your name; You are Mine... When you pass through the waters, I will be with you; And through the rivers, they shall not overflow you. When you walk through the fire, you shall not be burned, Nor shall the flame scorch you..."

God has His eye upon you, and you are precious to Him and loved. God is with you and doesn't want you to be in fear:

"Since you were precious in My sight, You have been honored, And I have loved you...
Fear not, for I am with you..."

God wants you to put your trust in Him—and Him alone:

"And My servant whom I have chosen, That you may know and believe Me, And understand that I am He. Before Me there was no God formed, Nor shall there be after Me. I, even I, am the Lord, And besides Me there is no savior..."

God is in absolute control:

"Indeed before the day was, I am He; And there is no one who can deliver out of My hand; I work, and who will reverse it?"

(Excerpts from Isaiah 43:1-13)

Worried Sparrows?

"Are not two sparrows sold for a copper coin? And not one of them falls to the ground apart from your Father's will. But the very hairs of your head are all numbered. Do not fear therefore; you are of more value than many sparrows." (Matthew 10:29-31)

If you ever see a lily toiling or a bird storing up food in a barn, then you will know that the time to worry has arrived.

The government (the rule and reign of your life) is upon *His* shoulder. He hasn't placed any of it on yours.

He has a plan and purpose for your life and He not only knows where He is taking you, but He also knows how to get you there.

The Government
shall be
UPON

His

shoulder.

(Isaiah 9:6 KJV)

The Healer of Hearts

To the saddened heart, He pours the oil of gladness;

To the discouraged heart, He brings a song of hope;

To the lonely heart, He comes with the nearness of His presence;

To the disappointed heart, He speaks a promise of better things;

To the drifting heart, He secures the anchor of His steadfast love;

To the wounded heart, He applies the healing ointment of His grace;

To the soiled heart, He washes with the rivers of His mercies;

To the troubled heart, He soothes with the quiet strength of His peace.

"He heals the brokenhearted and binds up their wounds [curing their pains and their sorrows]." (Psalm 147:3 AMPC)

Magnificence

"And all were astounded at the evidence of God's mighty power and His majesty and magnificence." (Acts 9:43 AMPC)

Only God can turn a life from:

Meaninglessness to *purposefulness,*

Barrenness to *fruitfulness,*

Heaviness to *joyfulness,*

Ugliness to *loveliness,*

Aimlessness to *hopefulness,*

Anxiousness to *peacefulness.*

These, and so much more, all declare His magnificence!

He is True!

"Even if everyone else is a liar, God is true. As the Scriptures say about Him, 'You will be proved right in what You say.'"
(Romans 3:4 NLT)

Either God is all-powerful or He is not...If He is not, we are sunk; If He is, we have nothing to fear.

Either God is all-knowing or He is not...If He is not, we'd better figure out what is best for us; If He is, we can be confident He will not make a mistake with our lives.

Either God is all-present or He is not...If He is not, we need to find a way to protect and take care of ourselves; If He is, we can be assured His eye is upon us, His hand is upon us, and the covering of His wings is over us.

Either God is the Father of mercies or He is not...If He is not, we should work hard to find a way to appease His wrath; If He is, we can, by faith, receive the forgiveness He's provided for us through the shed blood of His Son, Jesus Christ.

Come to the Waters

Let us move, with trusting hearts, into the lush, green meadow of His will; Let us graze upon the promises that keep our souls from want; Let us listen to the voice of the Shepherd who never speaks an uncaring word; Let us drink of the waters that quench our deepest thirst; Let us simply and peacefully walk upon the pathway of good things; Let us be refreshed within the resting places that He prepares for us along the way.

"Now on the final and most important day of the Feast, Jesus stood, and He cried in a loud voice, 'If any man is thirsty, let him come to Me and drink!'" (John 7:38 AMPC)

You See Him

He is the God of the mountain top and the valley.

On the mountain top you see Him as the God of all glory; *In the valley you see Him as the God of all comfort.*

On the mountain top you see Him as the Lord who reigns; *In the valley you see Him as the Shepherd who walks beside you.*

On the mountain top you see Him as the Lord God omnipotent; *In the valley you see Him as your loving Heavenly Father.*

"Show me Your ways, O Lord; Teach me Your paths." (Psalm 25:4)

The Only One

Let Him be the One:

You call upon...
"I will call upon the Lord, who is worthy to be praised; So shall I be saved from my enemies." (Psalm 18:3)

You wait upon...
"But those who wait on the Lord Shall renew their strength." (Isaiah 40:31)

You feed upon...
"I am the Bread of Life [that gives life—the Living Bread]. I [Myself] am this Living Bread that came down from heaven. If anyone eats of this Bread, he will live forever; and also the Bread that I shall give for the life of the world is My flesh (body)." (John 6:48, 51 AMPC)

You depend upon...
"We depend upon the Lord alone to save us. Only He can help us; He protects us like a shield." (Psalm 33:20 TLB)

Has He
EVER
forgotten you?
Will He
forget you
NOW?

"Can a mother forget her nursing child?
Can she feel no love for the child she
has borne? But even if that were
possible, I would not forget you!"
(Isaiah 49:15 NLT)

Rejoice!

This is the day the Lord has made. Love greeted you when you opened your eyes.

"To declare Your lovingkindness in the morning."
(Psalm 92:2)

Your day belongs to the Lord.

"My times are in Your hand." (Psalm 31:15)

Your theme song for the day is "Rejoice!"

"This is the day the Lord has made; We will rejoice and be glad in it." (Psalm 118:24)

Today is a fresh start in His mercies.

"The reason I can {still} find hope is that I keep this one thing in mind: the Lord's mercy... His compassion is never limited. It is new every morning. His faithfulness is great."
(Ecclesiastics 3:21-23 GW)

This is the day to live free from the cares of tomorrow.

"So don't ever worry about tomorrow."
(Matthew 6:34 GW)

Carry *hope in His promise* all through the day.

"Be zealous for the fear of the Lord all the day;
For surely there is a hereafter, And your hope
will not be cut off." (Proverbs 23:18)

P.S. At the end of the day, His faithfulness will be there to tuck you in at night.

"It is good to give thanks to the Lord, And to
sing praises to Your name, O Most High...And
Your faithfulness every night." (Psalm 92:1-2)

I Only Need You

I only need You, Lord, from the first light of dawn appearing in the eastern sky until the last golden hues of the sunset fade upon the western horizon. I only need You, Lord, when the night sky is over my head.

I only need You, Lord, when I rise up and when I sit down; when I go out and when I come in; when I am quiet and when I am active; when I am alone and when I am with others; when I am healthy and when I am ill; when I am up and when I am down; when I am on the go and when I stop to wait.

I only need You, Lord, when my lungs need to breathe; when my blood needs to flow, when my body needs to move; when my muscles need to work; when my mind needs to think, and when my heart needs to love.

I only need You, Lord, for as long as birds need flight, for as long as whales need the sea, for as long as clouds need moisture, for as long as wildflowers need raindrops, and for as long as sunflowers need the summer sun.

I only need You, Lord, for this present moment, for the moment when You take me home, for all the moments in between, and for all the moments ever after.

Because

I am not alienated,
Because *You love me.*
I am not unaided,
Because *You help me.*
I am not rejected,
Because *You are for me.*
I am not isolated,
Because *You are with me.*
I am not neglected,
Because *You care for me.*

I am not orphaned,
Because *You are my Father.*
I am not separated,
Because *You are my portion.*
I am not disheartened,
Because *You are my future.*
I am not unguarded,
Because *You are my defender.*
I am not alarmed,
Because *You are my God!*

"Thou openest Thy hand, and satisfies
the desire of every living thing."
(Psalm 145:16 KJV)

"Who considers these words enough? The hand of God being my chief provision and storehouse, is it not a shame to be anxiously careful for anything? Has the Lord all things in His hand? Then surely I shall receive what He has for me; none will be able to withhold it...you need not, says Christ, seek those other things; they shall be brought to you, if ye only abide in Me. If this does not comfort and strengthen us, nothing else will."

CARL BOGATZKY

Enjoy!

"Oh, taste and see that the Lord is good;
Blessed is the man who trusts in Him!"
(Psalm 34:8)

God is good to you! Enjoy the blessings that come from trusting Him.

His character is flawless, His worth is priceless, His power is endless, His faithfulness is ceaseless, His grace is boundless, His ways are blameless, His name is changeless, His blessings are countless, and His glory is fadeless.

"God also has highly exalted Him and given Him
the name which is above every name."
(Philippians 2:9)

His footsteps are your guidance;
call Him *The Way*.

His presence is your delight;
call Him *Wonderful*.

His truth is your foundation;
call Him *Rock*.

His will is your purpose;
call Him *Lord*.

His kindness is your comfort;
call Him *Shepherd*.

His promises are your hope;
call Him *Faithful*.

His riches are your supply;
call Him *Provider*.

His fellowship is your reward;
call Him *Life*.

His heart is your home;
call Him *Love*.

It's All About Him

"But whatever I am now, it is all because God
poured out his special favor on me—and not
without results. For I have worked harder
than any of the other apostles; yet it was
not I but God who was working
through me by his grace."
(1 Corinthians 15:10 NLT)

What we do is *for* the Lord... this helps
us understand our mission. All we do, we
do in obedience to His will and calling
upon our lives, and not because of our
ambition or personal agenda.

What we do is *unto* the Lord... this
helps us understand our motivation. All
we do is to please Him and bring Him
glory, instead of seeking to please others.

What we do is *with* the Lord... this
helps us understand our assignment. All
we do is as co-laborers with the Lord, and
not as independent servants.

What we do is *because of* the Lord... this helps us understand our stewardship. All we do is in His vineyard. It is His work and His ministry, not our ministry or our work.

What we do is *in* the Lord... this helps us understand our position. We serve from a place of rest and grace, and not from a place of striving or placing confidence in the flesh.

What we do is *by* the Lord... this helps us understand our source. All we have comes from Him, and without Him we would be empty vessels with nothing to give.

What we do is *through* the Lord... this helps us understand our effectiveness. We serve with the strength and the power which He supplies, understanding that it is not by human might or power, but by the Lord's Spirit that He does His work.

Who is Like Our God?

"You who have done great things; O God, who is like You?" (Psalm 71:19)

There is NO god like OUR GOD!

We don't need to help Him out, for He is *all-powerful;*

We don't need to give Him solutions, for He is *all-wise;*

We don't need to give Him explanations, for He is *all-knowing;*

We don't need to wake Him up, for He *never slumbers or sleeps;*

We don't need to hope that He will show up, for He is *always present;*

We don't need to try to figure Him out, for His ways are *past finding out;*

We don't need to make Him weapons of warfare, for He *knows no defeat;*

We don't need to try and get His attention, for His *ears are open* to our cry;

We don't need to be concerned about how He will take care of us, for He *is in control.*

"I am the LORD, and there is none else, there is no God beside me..."
(Isaiah 45:5 KJV)

Landscape

"And I am sure that God, who began the good work within you, will continue His work until it is finally finished on that day when Christ Jesus comes back again." (Philippians 1:6 NLT)

Life's like a landscape and God has the brush; His work is in progress, He's not in a rush.

❧

Each stroke has a purpose, and nothing's by chance; To learn of His wisdom takes more than a glance.

❧

The bird in the nest with its mouth opened wide, Is just a reminder that God will provide.

Now look at the sheep in the
meadow so green: The waters
nearby are both calm and
serene.

⌒~☙

The parts of the picture which
now seem unclear, Will take on
new meaning with each passing
year.

⌒~☙

Yes, God is still working in His
perfect way, As He paints the
landscape of your life each day.

Focus!

Not on the winds of opposition, but on the setting of the sail;

Not on the howling of the storm, but on the voice of the Captain;

Not on the darkness of the sea, but on the lighthouse on the shore;

Not on the density of the fog, but on the true north of the compass;

Not on the restlessness of the waves, but on the anchor that holds steady.

"God has given both his promise and his oath. These two things are unchangeable because it is impossible for God to lie. Therefore, we who have fled to him for refuge can have great confidence as we hold to the hope that lies before us. This hope is a strong and trustworthy anchor for our souls."
(Hebrews 6:18-19 NLT)

LORD,

I don't know

what will happen.

I don't know

what will be...but

TEACH ME

to LIVE *each* MOMENT,

with a HEART *that's*

worry free!

Still True

Grace still abounds;
Mercies are still new this morning;
Blessings are still being poured out;
Prayers are still being heard and
answered;
Promises are still being kept;
The love of God is still being shed abroad
in our hearts;
Angels are still ministering;
Jesus is still interceding;
The Holy Spirit is still working;
God is still on the throne;
The return of the Lord is still on schedule!

"Let the heavens rejoice, and let the earth be
glad; And let them say among the nations,
'The Lord reigns.'" (1 Chronicles 16:31)

You're Covered

Above you are the overshadowing wings;
   (Psalm 94:1)
Underneath you are the everlasting arms;
   (Deuteronomy 33:27)
Round about you is the angel of the LORD;
   (Psalm 34:7)
Beside you are still waters; (Psalm 23:2)
Within you is the peace that passes
   understanding; (Philippians 4:7)
Before you is the presence of the LORD;
   (Exodus 33:14)
Following you are goodness and mercy;
   (Psalm 23:6)
Ahead of you is heaven's home.
   (Philippians) 3:14-15.

EXPANDED FROM A QUOTE BY VIRGINIA BELL

Kept by the Keeper

"The LORD is thy keeper: the LORD is thy shade upon thy right hand." (Psalm 121:5 KJV)

As your keeper, God has no weaknesses and no place where He is vulnerable to attack. He is not helpless, defenseless, at risk, or in danger of a surprise attack.

Nothing and no one can lead to His downfall. It is impossible for God to be defeated. It is God who is your protector, shield, and fortress.

There is nothing that can separate you from Him in any battle. There is no separation between you and Your Captain, Your Warrior, and Your King.

You march under His banner; you advance under His command; you conquer with His sword; you stand upon His authority; you resist under His rule.

You are victorious because He is your victor; you are strong because He is your strength; you are an overcomer because He has overcome.

Gospel Power

"How beautiful are the feet of them that preach the gospel of peace, and bring glad tidings of good things!" (Romans 10:15 KJV)

It is only in the Gospel that we find God's power to change a life, make a heart new, and bring peace. Today, Jesus remains the only Savior from sin, the only Lord of life, the only King of Glory, and the only Prince of Peace. Let us wave His banner, sing His song, and celebrate His presence. He is the hope we carry in our hearts through every sunrise and sunset—until the coming of that brighter day, when His shout will be heard, the trumpet will sound, the Kingdom will come, the righteous scepter will be extended from His hand, and He will reign over all.

"Now may the Lord of peace Himself give you peace always in every way..." (2 Thess. 3:16)

Blessed
are all they
that put their
TRUST IN
HIM.

(Psalms 2:12)

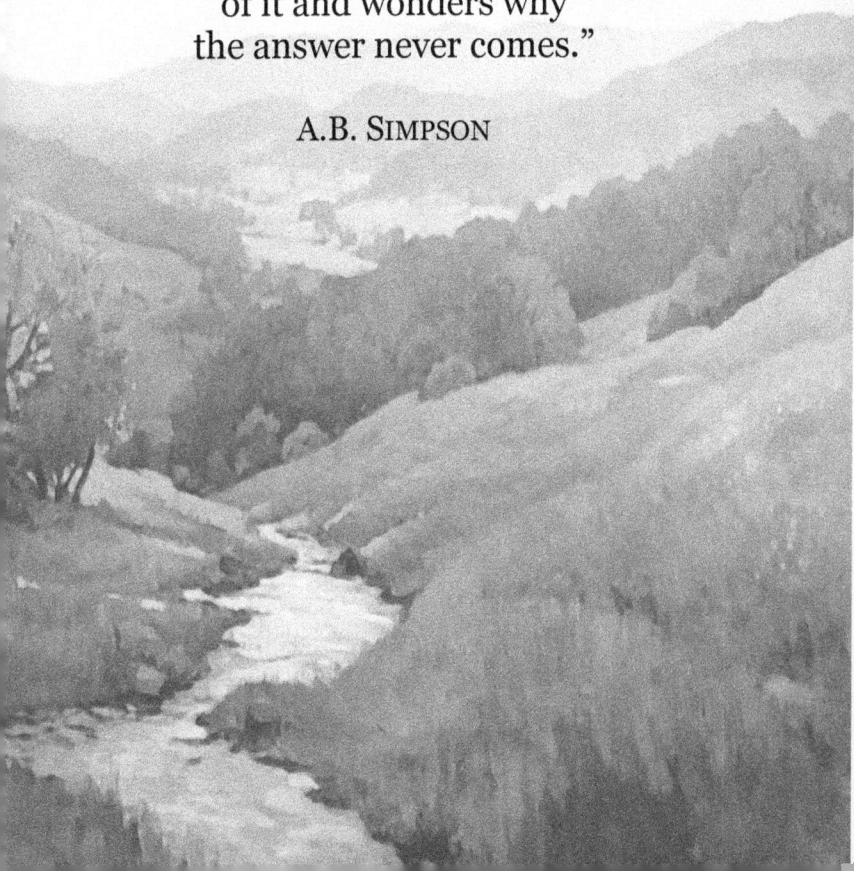

"TRUE FAITH
drops its letter in the
mailbox and lets it go.

"DISTRUST
holds onto a corner
of it and wonders why
the answer never comes."

A.B. SIMPSON

Dear Reader,

As kids growing up in New York City, there were times when we would run our hardest to get home before some bigger kids could beat us up. Once we were home, we knew we were safe.

To put your trust in the Lord is to go with all the strength in your legs and all the breath in your lungs, as quickly as possible, into the sheltered protection of the Lord. It's like your spirit is making a beeline for Jesus!

What a blessing it is to run to the Lord for protection. I pray these additional "trust" verses from the book of *Psalms* will help you to run to Him for shelter.

—Roy

Verses from
Psalms on

Trust

Psalms 4:5: Offer the sacrifices of righteousness, And put your trust in the LORD.

Psalms 5:11: But let all those rejoice who put their trust in You; Let them ever shout for joy, because You defend them; Let those also who love Your name Be joyful in You.

Psalms 7:1: O LORD my God, in You I put my trust; Save me from all those who persecute me; And deliver me...

Psalms 9:10: And those who know Your name will put their trust in You; For You, LORD, have not forsaken those who seek You.

Psalms 11:1: In the LORD I put my trust; How can you say to my soul, "Flee as a bird to your mountain"?

Psalms 16:1: Preserve me, O God, for in You I put my trust.

Psalms 17:7: Show Your marvelous lovingkindness by Your right hand, O You who save those who trust in You From those who rise up against them.

Psalms 18:2: The LORD is my rock and my fortress and my deliverer; My God, my strength, in whom I will trust; My shield and the horn of my salvation, my stronghold.

Psalms 18:30: As for God, His way is perfect; The word of the LORD is proven; He is a shield to all who trust in Him.

Psalms 20:7: Some trust in chariots, and some in horses; But we will remember the name of the LORD our God.

Psalms 25:2: O my God, I trust in You; Let me not be ashamed; Let not my enemies triumph over me.

Psalms 25:20: Keep my soul, and deliver me; Let me not be ashamed, for I put my trust in You.

Psalms 31:1: In You, O LORD, I put my trust; Let me never be ashamed; Deliver me in Your righteousness.

Psalms 31:6: I have hated those who regard useless idols; But I trust in the LORD.

Psalms 31:19: Oh, how great is Your goodness, Which You have laid up for those who fear You, Which You have prepared for those who trust in You In the presence of the sons of men!

Psalms 34:22: The LORD redeems the soul of His servants, And none of those who trust in Him shall be condemned.

Psalms 36:7: How precious is Your lovingkindness, O God! Therefore the children of men put their trust under the shadow of Your wings.

Psalms 37:3: Trust in the LORD, and do good; Dwell in the land, and feed on His faithfulness.

Psalms 37:5: Commit your way to the LORD, Trust also in Him, And He shall bring it to pass.

Psalms 37:40: And the LORD shall help them and deliver them; He shall deliver them from the wicked, And save them, Because they trust in Him.

Psalms 40:3: He has put a new song in my mouth—Praise to our God; Many will see it and fear, And will trust in the LORD.

Psalms 40:4: Blessed is that man who makes the LORD his trust, And does not respect the proud, nor such as turn aside to lies.

Psalms 44:6: For I will not trust in my bow, Nor shall my sword save me.

Psalms 49:6: Those who trust in their wealth And boast in the multitude of their riches...

Psalms 52:8: But I am like a green olive tree in the house of God; I trust in the mercy of God forever and ever.

Psalms 55:23: But You, O God, shall bring them down to the pit of destruction; Blood-thirsty and deceitful men shall not live out half their days; But I will trust in You.

Psalms 56:3: Whenever I am afraid, I will trust in You.

Psalms 56:4: In God (I will praise His word), In God I have put my trust; I will not fear. What can flesh do to me?

Psalms 56:11: In God I have put my trust; I will not be afraid. What can man do to me?

Psalms 61:4: I will abide in Your tabernacle forever; I will trust in the shelter of Your wings. Selah

Psalms 62:8: Trust in Him at all times, you people; Pour out your heart before Him; God is a refuge for us. Selah

Psalms 62:10: Do not trust in oppression, Nor vainly hope in robbery; If riches increase, Do not set your heart on them.

Psalms 64:10: The righteous shall be glad in the LORD, and trust in Him. And all the upright in heart shall glory.

Psalms 71:1: In You, O LORD, I put my trust; Let me never be put to shame.

Psalms 71:5: For You are my hope, O Lord GOD; You are my trust from my youth.

Psalms 73:28: But it is good for me to draw near to God; I have put my trust in the Lord GOD, That I may declare all Your works.

Psalms 91:2: I will say of the LORD, "He is my refuge and my fortress; My God, in Him I will trust."

Psalms 91:4: He shall cover thee with His feathers, and under His wings shalt thou trust: His truth shall be thy shield and buckler.

Psalms 115:9: O Israel, trust in the LORD; He is their help and their shield.

Psalms 115:10: O house of Aaron, trust in the LORD; He is their help and their shield.

Psalms 115:11: You who fear the LORD, trust in the LORD; He is their help and their shield.

Psalms 118:8: It is better to trust in the LORD Than to put confidence in man.

Psalms 118:9: It is better to trust in the LORD Than to put confidence in princes.

Psalms 119:42: So shall I have an answer for him who reproaches me, For I trust in Your word.

Psalms 125:1: Those who trust in the LORD Are like Mount Zion, Which cannot be moved, but abides forever.

Psalms 141:8: But mine eyes are unto thee, O GOD the LORD: in thee is my trust; leave not my soul destitute.

Psalms 143:8: Cause me to hear Your loving-kindness in the morning, For in You do I trust; Cause me to know the way in which I should walk, For I lift up my soul to You.

Psalms 146:3: Do not put your trust in princes, Nor in a son of man, in whom there is no help.

My Notes

_____

_____

_____

_____

_____

_____

_____

_____

_____

_____

_____

* 9 7 8 1 7 3 5 6 3 4 5 9 3 *